DK ANNABEL KARMEL

Find out what I make
with these ingredients
on pages 34–35

The Toddler
COOKBOOK

DK

LONDON, NEW YORK,
MELBOURNE, MUNICH, and DELHI

Design Rachael Foster, Hedi Gutt
Project Editor Carrie Love
US Editor Margaret Parrish
Photography Dave King
Food stylists Libby Rea
and Katie Rogers
Publishing Manager Susan Leonard
Category Publisher Mary Ling
Production Editor Sean Daly
Jacket Designer Hedi Gutt
Jacket Editor Mariza O'Keeffe

First published in the United States in 2008 by
DK Publishing
375 Hudson Street
New York, New York 10014

08 09 10 10 9 8 7 6 5 4 3 2 1
MD424—11/07
Copyright © 2008 Dorling Kindersley Limited

A catalog record for this book is
available from the Library of Congress.

ISBN 978-0-75663-505-3

Color reproduction by MDP, Great Britain
Printed and bound by Toppan, China

Discover more at
www.dk.com

Contents

4-5 Introduction

6-7 Things you will need

8-9 Mini Caesar salad

10-11 Lettuce boats

12-13 Easy cheesy bread rolls

14-15 Little pitta pizzas

16-17 Cherry tomato sauce

18-19 Chicken dippers

20-21 Chicken satay skewers

22-23 Salmon fishcakes

24-25 Corn quesadillas

26-27 Have a cooking party

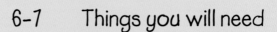

28-29   Party time!

30-31   Multicolored meringues

32-33   Tropical ice pops

34-35   Mini banana muffins

36-37   Peanut butter bears

38-40   Cutout cookies

41   Artist's fruit palette

42-43   Munchy oat bars

44-45   Mini lemon cheesecakes

46   Homemade lemonade

47   Fruit skewers

48   Index

Introduction

Cooking is lots of fun. The best way to learn is by watching Mom or Dad, but here are a few tips to help you make the recipes in this book.

When you have tried out the recipes, it's a great idea to invite a group of friends over for a cooking party where you make a meal together. You could even have your own restaurant at home—write out a menu, take orders, and serve a meal to the grown-ups. Or how about you and your guests preparing the yummy treats for a birthday party? Enjoy making the recipes, but most of all... enjoy eating the food!

Annabel Karmel

Kneading dough

To knead, use the heel of your hand to squash the dough away from you. Then fold the top end over toward you and give the dough a quarter turn clockwise. Keep going until the dough turns smooth and silky.

Grating and crushing

Grating cheese
Run a block of cheese down the side of the grater. Grate Parmesan against the small holes and Cheddar on the bigger holes.

Be careful of your fingers!

Grating ginger
Scrape off the skin with the tip of a teaspoon, then grate against the small holes. It's easier if you freeze the ginger first.

root ginger

Crushing garlic
Bash the garlic so it's easy to peel, then crush it with a garlic press or the back of a teaspoon.

Eggs

Eggs come in different sizes and I usually use the medium size in my recipes. When cooking with eggs, it's best to use them at room temperature.

TAP
TAP

Transfer the yolk from...

...one half shell to the other...

...letting the white run out.

Separating an egg is easy once you know how.
Have 2 bowls ready. Tap the egg firmly on the edge of one bowl so the shell cracks open. Let the egg white drop into one bowl and then tip the egg yolk into another bowl.

soft peaks

stiff peaks

overbeaten

Whisking egg whites
is easiest using an electric mixer (always ask Mom or Dad), but try it with a hand whisk.

There are 3 stages to whisking egg white. At the first stage, the whites form soft, floppy peaks when the blades are lifted up. Continue whisking and they will form stiff peaks that stand straight up, perfect for meringues. If you whisk the egg for too long it becomes lumpy and overbeaten.

Using ring molds is a good way to make my
mini lemon cheesecakes, since it shows the layers. Before using them, lightly grease the insides since this makes the cheesecakes easier to release.

Removing the ring

Run a knife around the inside edge to release the cakes. It helps if you rinse the knife in cold water after removing each cheesecake.

Melting chocolate
To do this on the stove, put a bowl over a pan of hot water, making sure the bowl doesn't touch the water. Leave for a minute then stir until all the chocolate has melted. Keep at room temperature.

Things you will need...

Do you recognize all the things in this picture?
You will be using them to make these recipes.

Oven temperatures are given in °F and °C.

For fan-assisted ovens, reduce the temperature by about 25°F (15°C).

To preheat the oven, allow at least 10 minutes for it to reach baking temperature.

...an apron

You're bound to get sticky hands but try to keep your clothes clean by wearing an apron.

egg whisk

melon scoop

hand beater

small strainer

blender

big strainer

plastic wrap

baking parchment

aluminum foil

small saucepan

mixing bowls

electric hand mixer

ring mold

8 in (20 cm) cookie sheet

rolling pin

ice-pop mold

lemon squeezer

cookie cutters

ice-cube mold

Things to remember

- **Wash your hands** before cooking and when you have been handling raw meat.
- **Wash fresh vegetables** and fruit before you use them in your recipe.

Being careful

- **Hot ovens and burners** require an adult, so watch or help on these steps.
- **Electrical equipment** and sharp knives must be handled by an adult.

...measuring things

Your numbers skills will help you to measure out the ingredients. You can use weighing scales, and measuring cups and spoons.

masher

garlic press

Ask an adult to help you grate ingredients.

box grater

colander

rolling pin

mallet

wooden spoon

palette knife

whisk

spatula

weighing scales

frying pan

mini-muffin pan

cookie sheet

cutting board

measuring cups

measuring spoons

piping bag and tips

cooling rack

Mini Caesar salad

The croutons are so *yummy* that you may want to make double and use the extra ones in soup.

You will need:

For the croutons
- 3 tbsp (30 g) Parmesan cheese
- 2-3 slices of white bread

For the dressing
- $1/2$ small clove garlic (optional)
- 6 tbsp mayonnaise
- $1/4$ tsp lemon juice
- 4-5 drops Worcestershire sauce
- 2 tbsp cold water

For the salad
- 2 hearts of romaine or 4 small bibb lettuces, leaves washed ` and dried.

Makes 4 main-course portions

How to make it...

Ask an adult to help.

1 Grate the cheese
Grate the Parmesan cheese using the fine side of a box grater. Be extra careful!

2 Make the croutons
Take 2-3 slices of white bread and cut into small star and heart shapes using mini cutters.

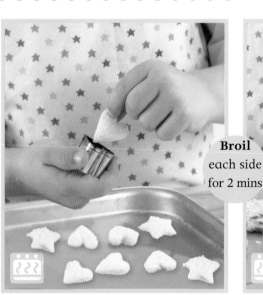

3 Arrange on a tray
Arrange the small bread shapes on a cookie sheet, then toast under the broiler.

Broil each side for 2 mins

4 Sprinkle with cheese
Sprinkle 2 tbsp of the grated Parmesan over the toasted croutons, ready to broil again.

Broil for 1-2 mins

5 Make the dressing
Crush the garlic (see p. 4). Put it in a salad bowl with the other dressing ingredients and remaining Parmesan.

Try it...
with chicken

Griddle 2 chicken breasts
that have been marinated
for an hour in olive oil, a
little lemon juice, and a
clove of crushed garlic.
Slice and scatter
over the salad.

or add bacon
Broil 8 strips of bacon until
crisp. Crumble and scatter
over the salad.

6 Add the lettuce

When the dressing is mixed together, season
with salt and pepper. Then add the lettuce leaves,
tearing the bigger ones into smaller pieces.

7 Mix it all up

Toss the lettuce leaves in the dressing.
Scatter over the croutons and serve.

Lettuce boats

These tasty fillings would also be delicious inside a wrap.

You will need:

- 2 oz (50 g) sliced, cooked chicken
- 3 tbsp drained, canned corn
- 1 sliced scallion
- 2 tbsp mayonnaise
- $1/4$ lemon
- 4-6 bibb lettuce leaves

Makes 4-6 boats

How to make them...

1 Tear the chicken

Tear the cooked chicken into little shreds using your fingers. Put in a bowl.

2 Add other ingredients

Mix in the canned corn, sliced scallion, and mayonnaise, plus a little pepper to taste.

3 Add lemon juice and mix

Add a squeeze of lemon juice ($1/4$ tsp) and stir.

Try this tuna mix

Mix together 2 tbsp mayonnaise, 1 tbsp ketchup, and a squeeze of lemon juice. Then add 1 can (6 oz/185 g) drained tuna (lightly mashed), 2 sliced scallions, 2 tbsp diced red pepper, and 2 tbsp of drained, canned corn.

4 Fill the lettuce boats

Spoon the filling into nice curly, boat-shaped lettuce leaves.

Chicken and beansprouts

Mix together 2 tbsp mayonnaise, 2 tsp plum sauce, and a squeeze of lemon juice. Then add a handful of beansprouts and 2 oz (50 g) sliced, cooked chicken.

Make a sail from a napkin and a toothpick

Easy cheesy bread rolls

There is nothing like the taste of fresh bread! Bake these *yummy rolls* for your lunch.

You will need:

- 1 envelope (¼ oz/ 7 g) fast-acting yeast
- 1 tsp sugar
- ⅔ cup (150 ml) warm water
- ½ cup (55 g) aged Cheddar cheese
- ½ cup (30 g) Parmesan cheese
- 1⅔ cups (225 g) white bread flour, plus extra for dusting
- ¼ tsp salt
- 1 tbsp sunflower or olive oil
- 1 egg
- sesame seeds, sunflower seeds, pumpkin seeds, and poppy seeds

Makes 8 rolls (or 16 mini rolls)
Bake at 400°F/200°C

How to make them...

1 Start with yeast
Put the yeast in a small bowl with the sugar. Add 3 tbsp (50 ml) of water and stir to dissolve the yeast. Leave to stand for 5 minutes.

Ask an adult to help.

2 Grate the cheese
Meanwhile, grate the Cheddar cheese on the large holes of a box grater, and grate the Parmesan using the fine holes. Be careful!

3 Mix flour and yeast
Put the flour in a large bowl and stir in the salt. Make a dip in the center and add the oil and the yeast liquid (this should be frothy).

4 Make into dough
Add the rest of the water and mix to a soft dough. Add a teaspoon of extra water if the dough is dry.

How to knead, p. 4

5 Knead until smooth
Turn onto a floured surface and knead until smooth—this will take about 10 minutes. Use the heel of your hand to work the dough.

6 Pat dough in circle

Pat the dough out into a circle about 8 in (20 cm) across. Spread the grated cheeses over it, then fold the dough in half.

7 Fold in the cheese

Fold in half again, so that the cheese is enclosed. Knead for 1-2 minutes more to work in the cheese.

8 Make into balls

Divide the dough into 8 pieces (or 16 for mini rolls) and form each one into a ball. Put on a lightly oiled cookie sheet, about 2 in (5 cm) apart, and press down slightly.

Try this...

Add sliced, sun-dried tomatoes to the dough at step 6. You could also make animal-shaped rolls.

Bake the rolls for 12–14 minutes.

Leave to rise

Cover with a damp dish towel and leave in a warm, draft-free place for 40-45 minutes. The rolls are ready to bake when they are roughly double their original size. Preheat the oven after around 35 minutes.

9 Brush with egg

Beat the egg with a pinch of salt. Uncover the rolls and brush the tops with a little of the beaten egg. Sprinkle them with seeds, then put them in the oven.

Little pita pizzas

Everyone loves pizza so why not have a party where the guests design their own pizza faces.

How to make them...

You will need:

- 1 small or half a medium red onion
- 1 tbsp olive oil
- 1 small garlic clove, crushed
- 1 tbsp tomato paste
- 2 tsp ketchup
- 1 tbsp hot water
- 2 small round pitas (or 1 large)
- $1/2$ cup (50 g) Cheddar cheese

Plus toppings of your choice (see opposite for ideas)

Makes 4 mini pizzas

1 Make the tomato base

Chop and fry the onion in oil for 5 minutes on medium heat. Add the garlic and cook for 1 minute. Stir in the tomato paste, ketchup, and water.

The pitas are easier to split if warmed a little first.

2 Split the pitas

Split the pitas in half and toast lightly until crisp. Divide the tomato base between the pitas and spread out right to the edges.

3 Add cheese

Ask an adult to help you grate the cheese. Scatter the cheese over the tomato base.

Preheat the broiler to high

4 Now add topping

Choose your favorite toppings and place on top of the cheese. Try making a pattern or face.

Broil for 1-2 minutes until the cheese has melted

Cool slightly before eating

Toppings to try:

ham

canned corn

olives, black, sliced ones

tomatoes, little cherry ones

scallions, thinly sliced

sweet peppers, green, yellow, or red

15

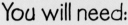

Cherry tomato sauce

Sweet cherry tomatoes make a tasty sauce that is good with any pasta.

How to make it...

You will need:

- 3 tbsp (30 g) chopped shallot (1 big shallot)
- 1 garlic clove
- 1 tbsp tomato paste
- $1/3$ cup (100 g) tomato sauce
- 2 cups (300 g) cherry tomatoes
- 2 tbsp olive oil
- 1 tbsp tomato ketchup
- 2-3 tbsp (50 g) mascarpone
- fresh basil leaves (4-5 big leaves)

Makes 4 small portions
Preheat oven to 350°F/180°C

1 Prepare ingredients
Dice the shallot, crush the garlic, and measure out the tomato paste and tomato sauce.

2 Halve the tomatoes
Wash the tomatoes. Then cut in half lengthwise and place on a cookie sheet lined with parchment.

3 Drizzle with oil
Drizzle 1 tbsp of the olive oil over the tomatoes. Then sprinkle with $1/4$ tsp salt. Now they are ready to roast.

Roast
for 20-30 minutes

Cut-side upward

4 Cook the shallot...
Cook the shallot gently in the remaining oil for 8 minutes, or until soft. Stir in the garlic and cook for another minute. Add tomato ketchup, paste, sauce, and roasted tomatoes. Bring to a simmer and cook for 10 minutes. Blend before you strain.

Try this!
Add strips of ham or halved black olives to the sauce.

5 Strain the tomato mixture

Strain the mixture over a bowl to remove the seeds and skins. You will need to press it through the strainer with a spoon.

6 Add the mascarpone

Stir the mascarpone into the sauce. Chop and stir in the basil leaves. You may want to add a little black pepper.

Pour your tomato sauce over cooked spaghetti and mix in. Delicious!

Chicken dippers

You can vary this by using your favorite flavored potato chips for the coating.

You will need:

- 2 chicken breast halves

For the marinade
- $^3/4$ cup (200 ml) buttermilk
- 1 tsp Worcestershire sauce
- 1 tsp soy sauce
- 1 small clove garlic, crushed
- $^1/4$ tsp paprika
- $^1/4$ tsp dried oregano

For the breading
- 5 oz (150 g) bag cheese-flavored potato chips
- 5 tbsp grated Parmesan cheese
- 6 tbsp all-purpose flour
- 1 egg

Makes enough for 4 people
Bake at 400°F/200°C

How to make them...

1 Make the marinade

Put the ingredients for the marinade in a large bowl and stir together until well mixed.

Wash hands after this

2 Coat the chicken

Cut the chicken into thin slices and coat in the marinade. Cover and refrigerate for an hour.

3 Crush the chips

Put the chips in a large bag and scrunch with your fingers, until they become small crumbs. Pour the crumbs onto a large plate and mix in the Parmesan.

4 Flour, then egg, then crumbs

Put the flour on a plate and mix in a little pepper. Beat the egg in a bowl with a tablespoon of cold water. Dip the chicken in flour, egg, then crumbs.

5 Put on a cookie sheet

Put onto a cookie sheet (no need to grease) and repeat until all the chicken strips are coated in crumbs. Bake in the oven for 15 minutes. Don't forget to wash your hands!

Meanwhile...

6 Make some dips

Mix the ingredients for each sauce in a small bowl, ready to dip your cooked crunchy chicken in.

Turn the chicken over halfway through the cooking time.

Allow to cool slightly before eating

Slightly spicy tomato
- $1/2$ tsp sweet chilli sauce
- 2 tbsp ketchup
- 2 tsp lime juice

Maple mustard mayo
- $1/4$ cup mayonnaise
- 1 tsp wholegrain Dijon mustard
- $1^1/2$ tsp maple syrup or honey
- 1 tsp cold water

Chicken satay skewers

You could also make this with prawns (2 large raw prawns per skewer) or strips of beef.

You will need:

- 2 chicken breasts

For the marinade
- small piece of ginger
- 1 clove garlic
- juice of 1 lime, 1 tsp reserved for sauce
- 1 tbsp soy sauce
- 1 tbsp honey
- 1 tsp peanut butter (smooth)

Makes 10 skewers

For the sauce
- $^1/_3$ cup (100 g) peanut butter (crunchy)
- $^1/_3$ cup (75 ml) coconut milk
- $^1/_3$ cup (75 ml) water
- 1 tbsp sweet chilli sauce
- 1 tsp soy sauce

Soak the skewers in water for 30 minutes to keep them from turning black when broiled.

How to make them...

1 Mix the marinade

Peel and grate the ginger ($^1/_4$ tsp), crush the garlic, and put in a bowl along with the lime juice, soy sauce, honey, and peanut butter. Whisk together.

2 Bash the chicken

Put the chicken breasts in a sealable plastic bag. Use a mallet or a rolling pin to bash the chicken breasts until they are about $^1/_4$ in ($^1/_2$ cm) thick.

3 Marinate the chicken

Slice each chicken breast into 5 strips and toss in the marinade. Leave for 10 minutes. Wash your hands.

Preheat the broiler to high

4 Make the satay sauce

Meanwhile, make the sauce. Put the peanut butter, coconut milk, water, sweet chilli sauce, and soy sauce in a small pan. Warm gently, stirring constantly, until everything has melted. Simmer for 1-2 minutes until the sauce thickens. Remove from the heat, then stir in 1 tsp of the leftover lime juice and set aside.

Dip the chicken in the sauce

5 Thread and cook the chicken

Thread the chicken strips onto skewers and put on a foil-lined cookie sheet. Wash your hands well. Broil for 5 minutes, then turn and broil for another 5 minutes until the chicken is cooked through.

Salmon fishcakes

These delicious little fishcakes will be swimming off your plate in no time.

How to make them...

You will need:

- 1 can pink salmon
- 2 medium scallions
- 2 tsp lemon juice
- $1/2$ tbsp mayonnaise
- $1/2$ tbsp ketchup
- 1 cup (40 g) fresh breadcrumbs
- 2 tbsp all-purpose flour
- 1 egg (medium)
- $3/4$ cup (50 g) dried breadcrumbs
- 2 tbsp sunflower or vegetable oil

For the dip
- 2 tbsp mayonnaise
- 1 tsp lemon juice
- 1 tsp sweet chilli sauce

Makes 6 fishcakes

To make breadcrumbs: Pulse 2 slices of white bread (without crusts) in a food processor.

1 Flake, add, mix

Drain the liquid from the salmon, then put the salmon in a bowl. Mash lightly. Chop and add the scallions. Add lemon juice, mayonnaise, and ketchup and mix it all up.

2 Divide it up

Add the fresh breadcrumbs, then mix again. Divide the mixture into 6 and form into balls, pressing firmly together. Then gently flatten into round patties. Ask an adult to make some of these fish-shaped.

4 Finish and cook

On the fish-shaped fishcakes make a space for the eye with your little finger. Heat the oil in a nonstick frying pan and fry the fishcakes over a medium-high heat for $1^1/_2$ minutes on each side, until they turn golden. Blot on paper towels and cool slightly. Add a cooked, frozen pea for each eye.

3 Dip in flour, egg, then breadcrumbs

Put the flour on a plate. Beat the egg in a shallow dish and put the dried breadcrumbs on another plate. Take each fishcake, dust it with flour, then dip it in egg, and coat with breadcrumbs. Wash your hands.

Sweet chilli dip

While the fishcakes cool, mix the dip ingredients together in a small bowl.

You can serve these with a few fries or simply on their own with the dipping sauce

Corn quesadillas

These make a super-tasty, quick supper.
They will soon become a favorite dish!

How to make them..

You will need:

- 1 small red onion
- $1/2$ red or orange pepper
- 7 oz (198 g) canned corn
- 1 cup (100 g) Cheddar cheese
- 1 tbsp olive oil
- 1 tbsp balsamic vinegar
- 1 tbsp honey
- 4-5 flour or corn tortillas
- $1/4$ cup salsa

Makes 4-5 quesadillas

You can use **mild or medium** salsa

1 Prepare ingredients
Chop up the red onion and the pepper, drain the canned corn, and ask an adult to help you grate the Cheddar cheese.

Did you know that quesadillas (pronounced ke-sah-dee-uh) are a Mexican dish?

24

2 Stir, stir, stir

Heat oil in a pan and stir-fry onion and pepper for 3 minutes. Add corn and cook for 2 minutes until the onion and pepper are soft. Add vinegar and honey—after 1 minute remove from heat.

3 Spread the mixture

Spread half of each tortilla with a heaped tbsp of salsa. Then add some of the corn mixture.

Preheat the broiler to high

4 Sprinkle the cheese

Scatter a little cheese over the salsa and corn mixture. Make sure you don't use too much since you will need some cheese to put on top of each tortilla.

5 Roll and cook

Roll the tortillas up and put on a cookie sheet. Scatter over the rest of the cheese. Broil the quesadillas for 1-2 minutes until the filling is hot and the cheese topping is lightly golden.

Have a cooking party

If you like cooking and you like having parties, why not do both at the same time? Invite a few friends and make some of your favorite recipes together.

Peanut butter bears
1 Put the puffed rice cereal in a bowl. Add confectioners' sugar and sesame seeds.
2 Melt the peanut butter and butter in a pan. Add to the bowl and stir in.
3 Divide the mixture into 8 and mix each portion together with your hands.

Cutout Cookies
1 Beat the butter, sugar, vanilla extract, and egg together.
2 Sift in the flour and add the salt. Mix again to make a dough.
3 Press the dough together to make a ball.
4 Roll the dough out, then chill for 30 minutes.
5 Cut out shapes using cookie cutters.

Make some recipe cards

Ask an adult to write out the recipes. The steps need to be clear. You can help decorate the cards.

Use both sides of the recipe card.

Please come to my
Cooking Party
Alfie

What you need to do

1. **Decide how many people** are coming. It's best to work in pairs, so go for even numbers.

2. **Choose your recipes**, then make a list of the ingredients you need.

3. **Borrow equipment** from friends if you do not have enough utensils, cookie sheets, etc.

4. **Make invitations** to mail or give out to your friends.

5. **Make recipe cards** with easy steps to follow. You can read through the steps together before you start.

6. **Prepare the ingredients** before everyone arrives. You could measure them out into small bowls or plastic bags.

7. **Find volunteers** (maybe moms or dads) to help out on the day.

Create your own invitations

Tie tags to wooden spoons for your invitations and give these out to your friends. These can be simple squares of colored paper or special cutout shapes.

Tell your friends to bring their spoons to the party

Attach the tags with colorful ribbons

To Luella
Please come
to a
Cooking Party
on
May 8
at
my house
love Millie x

To Luella
Please come
to a
Cooking Party
on
May 8
at
my house
love Millie x

Please come to my
Cooking Party
Sam

Please come to my
Cooking Party
Alfie

Please come to my
Cooking Party
Lewis

Please come to my
Cooking Party

To Luella
Come to a
Cooking Party
on
May 8
at my house
love   Millie x

Cookie cutters come in lots of wonderful shapes. Draw around them on card, then cut out and write your message.

Don't forget to take photos of your cooking party!

27

Party time!

Decorate a room for your party. When you've finished cooking you can sit down to eat your homemade treats.

Which pizza was yours? Did it have a funny face?

Mini pizzas and cutout cookies are party favorites and fun to make.

In between recipes or while your food is baking...

...or when you have finished eating, you can **play some games.**

Ready, set, GO!

Party games

Empty a few bags of colorful candies into a large bowl. Use straws to suck up as many as you can in one minute. Put the ones you win on a plate or piece of paper.

Something to take home...

Party bags

When you have decorated your cookies and peanut butter bears put a few into little clear bags for your friends to take home and enjoy.

Multicolored meringues

Choose any colors you like, but use the food coloring sparingly, one drop at a time.

How to make them...

You will need:

- 3 egg whites (medium)
- $3/4$ cups (150 g) superfine sugar
- $1/2$ tsp cornstarch
- $1/2$ tsp lemon juice
- Food coloring–red, green, yellow
Use a toothpick to add one drop at a time.

Makes 30 meringues

Bake at 250˚F/130˚C

1 Separate the eggs

Crack the eggs over a large bowl and separate the whites from the yolks (how to separate, see p. 5). You only need the whites.

2 Whisk the whites

Whisk the egg whites to stiff peaks. Be careful not to overbeat, since they will start to look lumpy, a little like cotton balls (see p. 5).

3 Add the sugar

Add one tbsp of sugar to the egg whites; whisk. Pour in a second and continue whisking. Add remaining sugar, while whisking to stiff peaks.

4 Add lemon juice...

Whisk in the cornstarch and lemon juice until just combined. The meringue should look smooth and glossy.

5 Add a little color

Divide the meringue into 3 bowls and color each one with a couple of drops of food coloring. Fold the color in using a spatula.

Piping tips:
To fill the piping bag stand it in a tall glass and fold the edges down over the rim.

For the swirls, use a ½ in (13mm) tip.

Serving suggestion

When the meringues are cool, sandwich them together with whipped cream or softened vanilla ice cream.

Try this... Just swirl the food coloring through the meringues a bit to get a marbled effect

6 Make meringue swirls

Spoon the meringue into a piping bag and squeeze to make swirls onto 2 cookie sheets lined with parchment. Make each one about 1 in (2.5 cm) across. Now bake in the oven.

Bake the meringues for 30-35 minutes, until firm on the outside. Turn off the oven and leave them for a further 45 minutes. Remove from the oven and cool.

Tropical ice pops

Make this refreshing frozen Pina Colada on a stick. It's delicious!

You will need:

- 1 lb (430 g) canned crushed pineapple in natural juice
- $1/3$ cup (85 g) superfine sugar
- $1/2$ cup (120 ml) coconut milk
- 1 large lime

Makes about 6-8 ice pops

How to make them...

2 Add lime
Squeeze the lime and add 2 tbsp of juice to the mixture. Mix again.

3 Fill the molds
Pour into ice-pop molds. Leave a little room at the top.

1 Put in a blender and mix until smooth
Put the pineapple, sugar, and coconut milk in a blender.

4 Put the lids on...
...and add the ice-pop sticks.

Ready
for
the freezer

To remove the frozen ice pop from the mold, run   warm water over it.

Freeze until
firm—at least
6 hours, but
best overnight

Make some mini ice pops

Pour some of the mixture into
small ice-cube molds (a rubbery
type is best for easy removal).
Freeze for around 2 hours, until
almost firm. Insert small wooden
skewers or toothpicks and freeze
again until solid.

To make: 30 minutes To bake: 12-14 minutes

Mini banana muffins

These mini banana muffins are made with tasty wholesome ingredients. They are just perfect for little fingers.

How to make them...

You will need:

- 1 medium egg
- $^1/_3$ cup (55 g) packed soft light brown sugar
- $^1/_2$ tsp vanilla extract
- 1 large, very ripe banana
- $^1/_4$ cup (55 ml) sunflower or vegetable oil
- $^2/_3$ cup (85 g) whole wheat flour
- $^1/_2$ tsp baking powder
- $^1/_2$ tsp baking soda
- pinch salt
- $^1/_4$ tsp ground cinnamon

Makes 18 muffins

Preheat oven to 350˚F/180˚C

1 Line the pans
Line 2 mini-muffin pans with 18 mini-muffin liners.

2 Mix egg and sugar
Crack the egg into a large bowl, then add the brown sugar.

3 Whisk together
Add the vanilla extract and beat together until thick.

4 Mash the banana
Break the banana into pieces in a small bowl, then mash it well with a fork.

5 Add to egg mixture
Add the mashed banana and the oil to the egg and sugar mixture.

Store in an airtight box for up to 3 days.

Try this!
Add a slice of banana or a sprinkle of sugar to the top

6 Sift the flour

Sift on the flour, baking powder, baking soda, salt, and cinnamon. Add any of the mixture left in the strainer to the bowl too. Stir together until just combined.

Fill the muffin liners

Spoon into the muffin liners (around two-thirds full). Then bake.

Bake for 12–14 minutes until risen and firm

Peanut butter bears

Great for a Teddy Bear's picnic, teatime treat, or birthday party.

You will need:

- 1$\frac{1}{3}$ cups (40 g) puffed-rice cereal
- $\frac{1}{3}$ cup (75 g) confectioners' sugar
- 2 tbsp sesame seeds
- $\frac{1}{3}$ cup (100 g) smooth peanut butter
- 3 tbsp (40 g) unsalted butter

To decorate
- 16 chocolate buttons or nonpareils
- mini colored candies
- black writing icing

Makes 8 bears

How to make them...

1 Add and stir
Put the puffed-rice cereal in a large bowl and stir in the confectioners' sugar and sesame seeds.

2 Melt and mix
Melt the peanut butter and butter in a pan over a low heat. Pour the mixture into the bowl and stir until everything is well mixed together.

3 Make into patties

Divide the mixture into 8 parts (roughly 2 tbsp each). Squish each one together with your hands, then roll each into a ball. Put the balls on a cookie sheet lined with parchment. Squish down slightly to flatten.

4 Decorate

Put chocolate buttons or nonpareils into the sides for ears and push in small colorful candies for eyes and noses. Use the writing icing to draw mouths.

Chill in the fridge for **30** minutes or until firm

Cutout cookies

It's fun to roll out dough and cut it into shapes.
Why not start a cookie-cutter collection?

How to make them...

You will need:

- 2 sticks (250 g) softened butter
- $^3/4$ cup (140 g) superfine sugar
- 1 egg yolk
- 2 tsp vanilla extract
- $2^1/2$ cups (300 g) all-purpose flour
- $^1/4$ tsp salt

Makes about 30 cookies

Bake at 350˚F/180˚C

1 Start mixing

Put the butter, sugar, egg, and vanilla extract in a large bowl and beat together until well mixed.

2 Add the flour

Sift in the flour and add the salt. Mix again to make a dough.

Chill the rolled dough in the fridge for 30 mins

3 Make into a ball

Now it's time to get sticky! Press the dough together firmly with your hands to make a ball.

4 Roll out the dough

Roll the dough between a folded piece of baking parchment. until about $^1/4$ in (5 mm) thick.

Turn the page for iced cookies

Press down firmly, making
sure the sharper side of
the cutter is facing down.

5 Press out shapes

Cut out shapes using cookie
cutters. Gather up the trimmings
into a ball, then roll out again and
make more shapes.

Mmm...
freshly baked
cookies!

Try this...

Make chocolate cookies
by splitting the dough
into two at step 3 and
adding 1 tbsp cocoa
powder to one half.

6 Put on a cookie sheet

Lift cookies with a palette
knife and arrange the shapes
slightly apart on nonstick
cookie sheets.

Bake
for about
14 minutes.
Then cool on
a rack.

Iced cookies

It's easy and fun to ice the cookies using tubes of writing icing. Choose your favorite colors.

Squeeze the tube gently and start decorating

Try adding edible silver balls.

Artist's fruit palette and dips

Be creative—use lots of different fruits to dip in these delicious sauces!

Lemon yogurt

Mix together

• 3 tbsp Greek yogurt
• 1 tsp milk
• 1 tsp confectioners' sugar
• 1 tbsp lemon curd

Raspberry-vanilla

Mix together...

• 3 oz (85 g) raspberries (fresh or frozen and defrosted)
• 1 1/2 tbsp confectioners' sugar
• 1 tbsp Greek yogurt
• 1/2 tsp lemon juice

...with a hand blender. Then strain to remove the seeds.

Tropical mango

Mix together...

• 1/2 large, ripe mango (3/4 cup (125 g) cubed flesh)
• 1 tbsp tropical fruit juice
• 1 tbsp confectioners' sugar

...with a hand blender. Strain if the mango has lots of fibers.

Chocolate orange

• 1 orange
• 2 oz (55 g) chocolate (use milk chocolate, broken into small pieces)

Grate 1/4 tsp orange rind into a bowl. Add 2 tbsp juice from the orange, then add the chocolate. Melt (see p. 5).

Chop some fruit...

...and get dipping!

Munchy oat bars

These oat bars are quick and easy to prepare, and they will give you lots of energy!

How to make them...

You will need:
- 3/4 stick (80 g) butter
- 1/2 cup (80 g) packed light brown sugar
- 3 tbsp (60 g) honey
- 1 1/2 cup (130 g) quick cook oats
- 1/2 tsp salt
- 4 large dried apricots
- 1/4 cup (35 g) raisins
- 1/4 cup (35 g) dried cranberries
- 1/3 cup (30 g) dried coconut
- 1/4 cup (30 g) pecans or pumpkin seeds

Makes 8 bars (or 16 squares)
Bake at 350°F/180°C

1 Melt the butter..
Put the butter, sugar, and honey into a saucepan and melt together over a low heat.

2 Add together
Put the rest of the ingredients in a large bowl. Snip the apricots with scissors; snap the pecan nuts.

3 Mix it all up

4 Add honey mixture
Pour the warm butter and honey mixture into the bowl.

5 Mix again
Now stir until everything is well mixed together.

Try different fruits and nuts in this recipe

6 Spoon into a baking pan

Line and grease an 8 in (20 cm) square baking pan. Spoon the mixture into the pan and press down with a potato masher to level the surface. Now it's ready for the oven.

Bake in a preheated oven for 20 minutes.

Cut into bars or squares when cool, then store in an airtight container.

43

Mini lemon cheesecakes

These are so deliciously lemony, you might want to make double quantities!

You will need:

For the base
- 5 graham crackers ($2^1/_2$ oz/70 g)
- $^1/_2$ stick (50 g) butter

For the lemony topping
- 4 tbsp Greek yogurt
- 6 tbsp lemon curd
- 1 tsp lemon juice
- $^1/_2$ cup (125 ml) heavy cream

To garnish (optional)
- blueberries or raspberries
- confectioners' sugar

Makes 4 cheesecakes in 3 in (7 cm) wide, 1 in (3 cm) deep ring molds. Lightly oil the inside of the molds.

How to make them...

1 Crush the crackers
Put the crackers in a plastic bag and crush them using a rolling pin.

Chill in the fridge while making the filling.

2 Melt the butter
Melt the butter in a small saucepan and stir into the crumbs.

3 Press into molds
Divide the crumbs into a selection of ring molds. Press firmly into the base, then chill.

4 Make the topping
Put the yogurt, lemon curd, and lemon juice into a large bowl and mix until smooth. In a smaller bowl, whip the cream until it makes slightly floppy peaks.

5 Fold in the cream

Mix 2 tablespoons of the whipped cream into the lemon yogurt mixture, then fold in the remaining whipped cream.

6 Spoon into molds

Spoon the lemon mixture carefully on top of the chilled bases. Fill to the top and smooth off with a palette knife.

Chill in the fridge for at least **30 minutes**, until firm

Garnish with **blueberries** and dust with confectioners' sugar

Try lime or orange curd instead of lemon curd.

Find out how to remove the ring mold on p. 5.

Homemade lemonade

It's refreshing on a hot day and packed with vitamin C!

Try pink lemonade
Just add a few drops of grenadine.

You will need:

- 1 cup (200 g) sugar
- 1/2 cup (150 ml) hot water
- 6 large lemons
- 1 1/2 pints (850 ml) chilled still or sparkling water

Makes 2 pints (1.25 liters)

How to make it...

1 Make the syrup
Put the sugar in a heatproof bowl and add the hot water. Stir to dissolve the sugar then set aside to cool.

Try fruity ice cubes

Put blueberries and tiny sprigs of mint in ice cube trays. Fill with water and freeze.

Add lemon slices and mint

2 Roll the lemons
This helps release the juice.

3 Squeeze the lemons
You need 8 fl oz (250 ml) of juice.

4 Add sugar syrup and chilled water
Pour the juice into a pitcher and stir in the sugar syrup. Add the water.

Fruit skewers

Make traffic-light fruit skewers with scoops of different colored melons.

How to make them...

You will need:

- 1 watermelon (red)
- 1 cantaloupe (yellow)
- 1 honeydew melon (green)

1 Make melon balls

Cut the melons in half and use a melon scoop to make balls of different colors.

2 Put on straws

Push a straw through the middle of the balls of melon. Remember the order is red, then yellow, then green.

47

Index

Bacon 9
Bread rolls 12-13

Canned corn 10-11, 14-15, 24-25
Cheese
    Cheddar 12-13, 14-15, 24-25
    Mascarpone 16-17
    Parmesan 8-9, 18-19
Cheesecakes 44-45
Chicken
    Caesar salad 9
    dippers 18-19
    lettuce boats 10-11
    satay skewers 20-21

Cookies 38-39, 40
Croutons 8-9

Dips
    chocolate orange 41
    lemon yogurt 41
    maple mustard mayo 19
    raspberry-vanilla 41
    satay sauce 21
    slightly spicy tomato 19
    tropical mango 41

Fruit
    32-33, 34-35, 41, 42-43, 45, 46, 47

Ice pops 32-33
Icing 36-37, 40

Meringues 30-31
Muffins 34-35

Oat bars 42-43

Pasta 16-17
Pizza 14

Quesadillas 24-25

Salmon fishcakes 22-23

Tuna 11

Annabel Karmel

Annabel is a leading author on cooking for children and has written 15 best-selling books that are sold all over the world.

She is an expert in devising tasty and nutritious meals for children without the need to spend hours in the kitchen.

Annabel writes for many newspapers and magazines and appears frequently on radio and TV as the UK's expert on children's nutritional needs. She has her own line of healthy foods for children in supermarkets.

Annabel was awarded an MBE in 2006 in the Queen's Honours List for her outstanding work in the field of child nutrition.

Visit Annabel's website at **www.annabelkarmel.com**

Other children's titles written by Annabel
Mom and Me Cookbook 978-0-7566-1006-7

Acknowledgments

With thanks from Annabel to: Caroline Stearns, Marina Magpoc, Letty Catada, Evelyn Etkind, and my children Nicholas, Lara, and Scarlett for testing the recipes with me.

Thanks to the models in this book: Tiana Baily, Mia Basford, Theo Cadby, Alfie Cooke, Luella Disley, Leah Fatania, Jasmin-Rae Germaine, Samuel James, Maisie Kemplin, Fred Manns, William Nichols, Daniel Price, Lewis Shamplina-Posner, Millie Sheppard, and Jasmine Teal.

Thanks also to Howard Shooter for photography on pages 42-43 (step sequence).